Genesis

A Small Group Bible Study Guide

PRESSED
THOUGHTS

GENESIS,
A SMALL GROUP
BIBLE STUDY GUIDE

Published by Pressed Thoughts LLC

www.pressedthoughts.com

21

ISBN 978-0-9850102-5-6

CONTENTS

INTRODUCTION TO THE GENESIS

Moses faced the same problem 3500 years ago that theology teachers face today.

Humans have an inherent need to understand our place in the world: to understand where we belong and to understand why we belong. Having such a defined place implies that the world must have order and, therefore, each of us in our own way synthesizes an order out of the facts and experiences we accumulate in our lives. This synthesis produces a set of beliefs that form the foundation of our sense of identity and, once formed, we subconsciously rebel against any facts or ideas that are counter to our already conceived notions. The problem, of course, is that humans have an amazing ability to synthesize information from incomplete evidence–an attribute that has helped us survive in a dangerous world but that also leaves us with an unreliable understanding of it. Most of us pass through life with a mixed set of misconceptions, but it is apparent from Genesis that God wants His people to have a clear conception of Himself and our relationship with Him.

So, the problem that Moses faced is that the nation he led out of Egypt had a muddled view of their identity: of where they belong, of why they belong, and perhaps more importantly, to whom they belong, and God had called Moses from a burning bush to lead this people into a new home and into a new understanding.

Genesis constitutes Moses' inspired attempt to begin this re-shaping of the Israelites' set of beliefs and resulting sense of identity. The remaining books of the Bible draw upon, re-enforce, and continue Moses' efforts in this area both correcting us as we drift away from what previous prophets taught us, and building upon these earlier revelations with new depths of understanding. When writers set out to change a world view, they need to share and expound their revolutionary ideas, but they also need to contradict, re-shape, or re-purpose the existing beliefs of their audience. The Israelites' world view, as they walked out of Egypt, was one shaped by four hundred years of cruel slavery: worthless servants of the Egyptian god kings. Genesis takes the form of a family history, but through this history, Moses interjects the revolutionary idea that this family is God ordained and, while doing so, re-shapes and re-purposes the local pagan theologies to reveal the true nature of our loving God as the sole author of life.

For the Israelites, being willing to doubt their old beliefs and learn from Moses took humility, and it is interesting to note the humility of the two most prominent men God chose as early instruments of his plan of redemption: Abraham (Gen. v. 18:27) and Moses (Num. v. 12:3). What was true then is still true now: prideful men are confident in their own set of beliefs and sense of identity and, because of this, lose their ability to absorb new ideas that may bring them closer to truth. Humble men, on the other hand, recognize the inherent limitation of themselves and others. They are willing to shift and mold their existing beliefs as they learn from God and are also willing to support and have patience with others as they struggle to do the same.

It would be fair to study Genesis, academically, as a historical narrative, a work of persuasive writing, or a theological treatise because it is all of these things. However, the value of this book comes when we don our own attitudes of humility, suspend any pre-conceptions given to us by past preachers and school teachers, and allow the words of Moses to re-shape and mold our own current world view to that of God's.

In some ways, it is easier for us to understand Genesis because we have already been given the rest of the story, but in other ways, it is harder because Moses was not writing for us, he was writing for his own people: the recently freed Israelite slaves of Egypt. In Exodus, we learn that God gave Moses the Law directly; however, the rest of the Pentateuch, starting with Genesis, was written through the inspiration of the Lord by a simple man using his own words and personality to fulfill the purpose God set for him, inaugurating a pattern that would continue until the coming of the Messiah.

Our western culture has an analytical mindset and way of thinking that can trace its roots to the ancient Greek philosopher Aristotle (~350 B.C.) and began to fully blossom with the philosophers and physicists of the Renaissance. Our natural disposition, when studying new material, is to invoke the rational scientific method of analysis and testing to help us understand it. Our minds have been sharpened by our teachers through endless hours of essay writing and mathematics homework. And since the advent of writing paper and the printing press (not to mention the Internet), we have benefited from the wisdom, knowledge, and ideas of the brilliant people before us, because we can read the very words they wrote. Our practiced analytical dexterity and raw foundation of knowledge is far beyond that of the ancient Israelites.

In 1500 B.C., the few who could write did so by chiseling stone, etching into soft clay, or scratching on the surface of pottery shards. For the vast majority of people, the entirety of a person's knowledge was limited to what they could remember of what their family and friends told them. There was no concept of writing yourself a note for later or looking something up online.

From generation to generation, knowledge was passed along orally by storytellers who used a number of memory techniques to help remember their tales, including the use of vivid imagery and detail, inclusion of geographic markers, repetition, and most especially, the use of rhyme. In fact, scholars of ancient storytelling tell us that most stories were conveyed as poetry or song, and from generation to generation, stories became naturally pruned, with the less memorable parts fading away. (Evidence of such storytelling can be readily scene in the book of Job, but vestiges can be inferred in parts of Genesis as well.) At the time, neither the storytellers nor their listeners had a notion that the facts of a story could be verified—they simply couldn't be, other than by asking a different storyteller. And when the facts aren't verifiable, the theme becomes the preeminent component of a story.

Understanding this radical difference between our patterns of thinking and the ancient Israelites' patterns of thinking is invaluable in understanding Moses' approach to writing. Had Moses been writing in our time, Genesis would open with an abstract, close

3

with a short bibliography, and contain succinct rational arguments to connect what we already know with the new ideas that he was presenting as well as logically constructed arguments to refute incompatible points that had been made in competing thesis. It would then be supplemented with a good smattering of charts, graphs, and bulleted lists. Of course Moses didn't write in our time, he wrote in a time of storytelling, and what he wrote was a story that these slaves, steeped in a specific pagan culture, could relate to. The Genesis story, then, is a bridge designed to lead a people from one set of false ideas, to a new set of ideas founded in Godly truth. In order to distinguish clearly, between the two sides of this bridge, it is necessary to understand the cultural beliefs of that time.

The Israelites' understanding of the world was almost certainly influenced by Canaanite mythological tales passed down through their four hundred years of captivity as well as by the mythology of the Mesopotamians, several hundred miles to the Northeast, but was likely most impacted by the Egyptian mythology of their day. A supplement describing the core ideas of this mythology appears later in this guide.

Through the stories in Genesis and the remaining books of the Pentateuch, we can see how God, through his servant Moses, led them across that bridge, transforming this seemingly forgotten and disconnected people into a new nation that would continue on to the days of Christ. While Moses was, indeed, writing to the Israelites of his own time, his words were inspired by God and are as relevant today as they were 3500 years ago. They still help us to understand who we are, who God is, and why our relationship with Him is so precious.

While Moses is generally credited with writing all five books of the Pentateuch, most of the more than 30 Biblical references to Moses' authorship more specifically refer to the *Law* (Deut. 3:9, Ex. 24:3-4, 2 Ch 33:8), and it is not clear whether or not these references to the Law were intended to included Genesis. However, references to Moses' prophecies of Jesus (John 1:45, 5:46), may have been referring to verses in Genesis such as v. 3:15 (*I will put enmity between you and the woman, and between your offspring and her offspring; he shall bruise your head, and you shall bruise his heel*) and v. 18:18 (*all the nations of the earth shall be blessed in him*). Given the nature of the family stories within Genesis, it seems reasonable to assume that many of these tales had been passed down to Moses' time through oral tradition and, given that Moses spent considerable time, face to face, in the tent of meeting with God Himself (Ex 33:7-11), Moses had ample opportunity to fact-check these stories. Further, the stories of Genesis are referenced by teachers and prophets throughout the Bible, including references by Jesus himself (John 8:56) and such references provide authority to this book.

Scholars, performing a textual analysis of Genesis, have noted three distinct styles of writing, possibly indicating that, as this scripture had been passed down through the generations, it underwent an editing and re-assembly process. One theory, (known as the JEPD theory), asserts that after the nation of Israel split in two (1 Kings 12), one version of the Genesis stories was edited in the southern kingdom of Judah and another version was edited in the northern kingdom of Israel. Text from the southern version can be distinguished from that of the northern through various textual elements, most notably the fact that the southern version (known as the *Yahwist* source) used *Yahwah* as the Lord's name, while the northern version (known as the *Elohist* source) used *Elohim*. Other elements, including the various genealogies, have originated from a third source, known as the *Priestly* source, according to JEPD.

No theory on the origin of Genesis is provable and no theory is universally accepted; therefore, it is reasonable to wonder if the versions of Genesis we have today are true. In 1978, a conference of evangelical scholars drafted *The Chicago Statement on Biblical Inerrancy* in which they declared their belief that all scripture is infallible and inerrant but only in the form that they were originally written (no original versions of any part of the Bible exist) and only when properly interpreted (and there is always disagreement on how to properly interpret).

We do have copies of Biblical manuscripts dating nearly from the time of Christ, and given the veracity of Bible scribes in insuring accuracy in their copying efforts, we can have confidence that no significant alternations to the text have occurred since the Apostle Paul wrote that *All Scripture is breathed out by God and profitable for teaching, for reproof, for correction, and for training in righteousness* (2 Tim. 3:16). And since the time of Jesus, Christians, bolstered through their knowledge of the scriptures, have brought healing change to the poor, to the weary, to the imprisoned, to the addicted, and perhaps to you as well. This evidence indicates that God's hand, through the centuries, has been in the creation of the

Bible version that we have today and, therefore, it is worthy to study so that we can grow. Scholars may debate the meaning of truth and error, the accuracy of historical and seemingly scientific statements within Genesis, and its authorship, but what they cannot dispute, is its effectiveness in achieving God's purposes, which is to change lives by bringing people closer to Himself.

While some argue about how Genesis may have been edited and transcribed as it passed down through history, few argue over the miraculous nature of it. Winston Churchill once said *History is written by the victors*, and most history books are filled with the courageous and virtuous deeds of their heroes. In page after page of Genesis, we see the failures of our spiritual ancestors in embarrassing detail. We see their lies, their deceit, their incestuous deeds, their disloyalty, and their murder. This pattern of raw transparency is echoed throughout the Bible, which causes one to wonder, who actually was the victor that authored this book? The answer should be obvious.

THE EGYPTION CREATION MYTHS

Archeologists, studying ruins in Egypt and surrounding lands, have uncovered tablets and other evidence of the early Egyptian's creation mythology. The evidence unearthed reveals a number of variations of some core mythological ideas. They were a polytheistic people and their gods existed as attributes or phenomena of the world, such as the Sun, Earth, and light. The variations from this core theme show different roles ascribed to different gods (e.g. in some accounts the primary creator god is Atum, others Rê, and in others Ptah), but the central ideas are the same. A somewhat simplified version of the ancient Egyptian creation mythology follows:

Before creation, there was nothing but an infinite, dark and empty sea. The creator god, creates himself as light in the dark waters and wind over the water's surface. He then creates the world by commanding the waters to separate, forming an atmospheric bubble in the waters. Once the atmosphere is created, he commands the earth to separate from the water, then commands the sun to rise up. In their understanding, the sun, moon, and stars float on the waters on the upper half of the atmospheric bubble. Once the sun is created, he creates the plants and animals and, finally, creates man, in his image, by forming him on a potter's wheel and animating him through his breath.

In some accounts, creation occurs through the act of naming, particularly the creation of other gods. In others, creation occurs through commanding that, in the Egyptian understanding, implied the notion of conceiving of an idea and then annunciating it. The fact that such an annunciation from either a god or a king came to fruition was a sign that the speaker was truly a ruler.

Creation, in the Egyptian myths, occurred in a single day. After satisfactorily completing the creation of all the lesser gods, along with towns and shrines for them, the creator god rests knowing the world is in proper order.

At the end of the day, the sun travels to the Egyptian underworld, known as Duat, where it battles chaos, in the form of a serpent. The process of creation then repeats itself again, the next day, with the sun once again rising up out of the lower waters.

NAMING IN THE ANCIENT NEAR EAST

Names, in the ancient near east worldview, contained the essence of a person's soul, conveying meanings and attributes that were binding on the named individual. Therefore, the one doing the naming had power over the one being named, and by changing a person's name, the ruler could change a person's destiny: the Lord changing the name of *Abram* (exalted father) to *Abraham* (father of a multitude), would have been significant to the people of the time.

Within the culture, there was also the idea that a name conveyed power and one could exercise power over another simply by knowing their name. (For this reason, within some tribes it was customary for a person to keep their real name secret and use an alias in public life.) This idea of a name conveying power can be seen in Deuteronomy 18:5 *For the Lord your God has chosen him out of all your tribes to stand and minister in the name of the Lord* and is also evident by Israel's fear of even uttering the name of the Lord.

In order to understand these scriptures in the way the early Israelites did, it is important to check the footnotes in a Study Bible to learn the meaning of the names of people and places and to take special note of when God had a hand in the naming.

TIMELINE OF THE PATRIACHS

The genealogies within Genesis are detailed, particularly in regard to people's ages, through Joseph. As evidenced by Matthew 1:1–17, and Luke 3:23–38, genealogy continued to be important to the Israelite nation up to the time of the destruction of the temple in 70 A.D., when the nation's genealogy records were lost. Using a much debated date of 1900 B.C. for Joseph's rise to power in Egypt, these genealogies have been used to produce the chart below. Using this timeline, the flood occurred in 2474 B.C., which corresponds to the death of Methuselah. Note also that Abraham was about 57 years old when Noah died.

	Lifespan	Age
Adam	4130-3200 B.C.	930
Seth	4000-3088 B.C.	912
Enosh	3895-2990 B.C.	905
Kenan	3805-2895 B.C.	910
Mahalalel	3735-2840 B.C.	895
Jared	3670-2708 B.C.	962
Enoch	3508-3143 B.C.	365
Methuselah	3443-2474 B.C.	969
Lamech	3256-2479 B.C.	777
Noah	3074-2124 B.C.	950
Shem	2571-1971 B.C.	600
Arpachshad	2471-2033 B.C.	438
Shelah	2436-2003 B.C.	433
Eber	2406-1942 B.C.	464
Peleg	2372-2133 B.C.	239
Reu	2342-2103 B.C.	239
Serug	2310-2080 B.C.	230
Nahor	2280-2132 B.C.	148
Terah	2251-2046 B.C.	205
Abraham	2181-2006 B.C.	175
Isaac	2081-1901 B.C.	180
Jacob	2021-1874 B.C.	147
Joseph	1930-1820 B.C.	110

THE SMALL GROUP BIBLE STUDY

The purpose of this guide is to support a small group Bible study of Genesis. It is designed to encourage the participants to think deeper about what they are reading, to learn how to draw out wisdom that can be applied to their own lives, and to see, through firsthand study, how the Bible, in its entirety, weaves together a tale of God's love for us.

An effective small group Bible study has multiple goals. One, of course, is to facilitate the mutual, intellectual understanding of the text under study. Another, more important aspect of the group, is to build closer relationships with one another. It makes no sense to mechanically lead a small group through a Bible study with steadfast determination. Sometimes it is important to take a break on this study of Christian love, so that the group can actually engage in Christian love. So as you move through the study, do not be afraid of tangential conversations and do not be afraid to even skip the scheduled study of the day if the Spirit is leading the group to spend a little time building intimacy or helping someone work through a life issue.

The chapters of this guide break the study of Genesis into five lessons according to general topic; however, the questions within these chapters follow the book chronologically to enable the group to set their own pace of study. As a group, it is important to adjust the pace of the lessons based on the level of discussion activity within each session.

The questions within this guide are designed to help reveal the great depth of wisdom that Moses is sharing as well as to help the group understand how this wisdom applies to their own life. It can be helpful, at the start or end of each session, to step back and review the main themes of the section discussed so that these primary points do not become obscured within the context of the more in-depth questions.

As you sit down to read the scriptures prior to each of these sessions, take the time to pray that the Holy Spirit guide you in your understanding of the text. And as you meet together as a group, pray for each other and pray that the Holy Spirit guide the discussion in a manner pleasing to the Lord.

HOW TO STUDY A BOOK OF THE BIBLE

A book of the Bible can be studied in many different ways and a student or study group is free to go to whatever depth of study they desire. On the shelves of bookstores, you can find that authors have written whole volumes focusing on just a single verse of the scriptures. Many have found that after they have read through and studied larger portions of the Bible at a higher level, their ability to understand each individual book is deepened. The converse is also true.

The style of this guide supports a discussion oriented study that should leave the student with a fair understanding of the main messages of the book. The questions in this guide look at the text from three perspectives, following a teaching tradition dating to the early church fathers. First, they lead the student to understand the text from the perspective of the original audience. Second, they reveal how passages in the Old Testament appear to pre-figure, and connect with, the events of the New Testament, and third, they help the student see how wisdom can be extracted from the text and applied to their own lives.

When extracting wisdom from the Bible, it is important to be cognizant of the fact that the Lord interacts with and has different expectations of people depending on their level of spiritual maturity, their personality, and the cultural environment in which they live. In Luke 1:20, the Lord strikes Zechariah mute for doubting the Lord, yet in Gen. 18:12, Sarah laughed at the Lord for virtually the same reason and the Lord did nothing. The difference, is that

Zechariah was a priest and the product of the Law of Moses and 2000 years of prophets: the Lord expected a high level of spiritual maturity. In contrast, Sarah had nothing more than oral legend to guide her knowledge of God; therefore, when extracting wisdom to apply in your own life, you must consider how the Lord interacted with the historical men and women in the Bible as well as your own spiritual maturity, personality, and cultural environment.

To understand the cultural background of Moses' original audience, it is very useful to first read the entire Pentateuch (Genesis through Deuteronomy), cover to cover, or at least Genesis and Exodus. Once you have this background knowledge, proceed with the lessons on Genesis, reading through each set of chapters again with more care. It is often helpful to make notes on what you perceive as the key points of the text. You can then read the questions within this guide, making notes and writing down answers as you go.

It is strongly recommended that a Study Bible be used for this study and in an edition that is readable for you. For Genesis, a cultural backgrounds study Bible may be particularly helpful. If you are very comfortable reading old English, or just like a challenge, then the King James version may be for you. The majority of scripture passages used in this book are from the ESV Bible, which was translated with a philosophy of making the text readable but, to the extent possible, maintaining the form of the original Biblical texts.

Take the time to learn the cross reference system used by your particular study Bible and especially note that Study Bibles are meant to be *dirty* Bibles. As you read along, don't hesitate to underline meaningful verses, scribble notes in the margin, and otherwise markup your Bible.

Other Bible resources are available to aid in the study and should be used freely to help you gain further insight. Digital versions of the Bible are available online and also available for handheld devices. These versions provide full-text word search capability that is ideal for locating and reading other passages of scripture that relate to the current study.

GENESIS 1–2:3

The Hebrew word, *Toledoth*, means an account, history, or genealogy, and the book of Genesis is a series of Toledoth's. (In fact, the very word Genesis came from a Greek translation of *Toledoth*). The Toldoth's are usually demarked by phrases such as that in Gen 5:1 *This is the written account of Adam's family line.* Most scholars see these phrases as the introduction of a Toledoth; however, some have argued that such phrases denote the conclusion of a Toledoth and might better have been translated as *This was the account passed down from Adam.* The structure of the Toledoths typically include an introductory summary of the account, followed by detail.

For the people of the 21st century, this first Toldeth, providing an account of creation, has generated more unanswered questions and controversy than perhaps any other story in the Bible. For all humanity prior to Darwin and Isaac Newton, the physical aspects of creation could be accepted at face value, leaving the hearers free to focus on the major theme of the story: the preeminence of the Lord God and His authority over all things.

1) Acts 17:22-29 describes how Apostle Paul introduced the gospel to the Greek people of Athens. What did Paul choose as the foundation for his exhortation? In Genesis 1 and 2, Moses begins his message to the Israelites. What did Moses use as the foundation for his message?

2) In Egyptian mythology, the culmination of creation was the sun god. According to Genesis, what is the culmination of God's creation (vv. 1:26-31)? In what ways, did Moses minimize the importance of the sun in his account? In Mesopotamian mythology, the gods created man to be slaves of the gods and relieve them of their labors. According to Moses, why did God create man?

3) Moses used unique phraseology in describing the days of creation in verses 1:3-2:3 (which was best translated in the NASB). The phraseology used for the first six days may best be interpreted as describing a collection of days, rather than a sequence of days. Why would Moses make a deliberate point of describing the act of creation as taking more than one day (refer to the introduction on Egyptian mythology)? The Egyptian mythology describes the creation process as battling the forces of chaos each night, followed by a repeated re-creation each day. How does this differ from Moses' account?

4) According to both Egyptian and Moses' descriptions, the creator rested after satisfactorily completing their creation. The Egyptian god's rest came to an end when the sun descended. How long did God's rest last (v. 2:1-3, Heb. 4:1-4)?

5) The Egyptian myths describe a world composed of many gods to serve and worship and also include the notion that the king serves as a tangible representative of god. How does this differ from Moses' account?

6) What purpose was Moses intending to achieve through the account of creation in Genesis 1 and 2 (refer also to Ex. 6:2-7, 9:14, 20:1-8). How successful was Moses (Ex. 32:1, Josh. 24:14-15)?

7) Why might the creation accounts from Canaan, Mesopotamia, and Egypt bear a resemblance to each other and to that of Moses (Gen. 10)?

8) What are the key points that God was trying to convey in Gen.

1-2:3? What are your own key takeaways?

GENESIS 2:4-4

The account of Adam and Eve provides the foundational backdrop of God's redemptive plan that culminated in Jesus' death and resurrection. The story is significant for both what it tells us and what it leaves out, and students of Genesis may be surprised to realize how many sermons they've heard have been based more on an interpolation of this story, than the story itself.

In these passages, we see the inauguration of pain and suffering in the world. Through one small, careless act of disregard of the warning from God, our relationship with our Father was lost and our role on earth changed forever. It would be easy for us to blame all our life's pain on Adam and Eve if we weren't so aware of our own disregard of God's warnings and wisdom.

This story, though, has two perspectives. The perspective of man is the one we focus on the most, because we have not yet fully shed the self-centered worldview of Adam. The other perspective, and one that we should not lose, is that of God's, which was filled with His painful anguish as He was forced to separate man from Himself. A painful anguish that He experienced again at Calvary as He enabled an the end of this separation.

1) What was significant about the fact that the Lord had Adam name the animals (see the introductory section on naming in the ancient near east culture)? Who named *Eve*, and what does *Eve* mean (vv. 2:23, 3:20)?

19

2) What two purposes did God put man in the garden to do (v. 2:15)? What can we learn about happiness from these two purposes?

3) There are two grand analogies that God has repeatedly used to help describe our relationship with Him. The second analogy describes God as a husband to His people (Isa. 54:5, 62:5, Jer. 3:14, Ezek. 23:37, Hos. 1:2, 2 Cor. 11:2, Rev. 19:7-9). Wisdom that the Bible shares about marriage is often useful in helping us understand our relationship with the Lord; likewise, Biblical wisdom on strengthening our relationship with the Lord can be applied to strengthening marriages. How is mankind's relationship with God similar to a wife's relationship with her husband? What responsibility does a husband have towards his wife (Prov. 31:28, Eph. 5:22-23, 1 Tim. 5:8, Col 3:19)? How does the Old Testament describe the role of a women in a marriage relationship (v. 2:18, Prov. 31:10-31)? Is there any shift in emphasis between these passages and descriptions of the role of women in the new Testament (Eph. 5:22-24, Col: 3:18)? At the time of Christ's ministry, had mankind's relationship with God shifted away from what it was originally intended to be? Would understanding this shift in emphasis help us understand how we might improve our relationship with the Lord?

4) The institution of marriage has existing throughout history and in nearly all cultures; however, its purpose has not enjoyed the same consistency. In some cultures, marriage has been used as a means of securing property rights, to broker peace between tribes, to extend a family line, or to create and raise a family (usually with the wife's role being to raise the children). Within the past fifty years or so, in western societies, marriage has meant companionship with someone you love, and the idea that your spouse should be your best friend. In your current society, what are the attributes of marriage? The story of Adam and Eve, as told in Genesis, provides the very template for this relationship that we call marriage, but it does so with very few words. What are the core attributes of marriage as described in Genesis?

5) The Hebrew word, *Dabaq*, used Gen 2:24, has been translated as *cleave*, *united*, *joined*, *hold fast*, or *cling* (this same word is used in Duet. 10:20, 11:22, & 13:4). What core concepts are implied by this word? What is God's intended duration of our relationship with Him? What is God's intended duration of a marriage? Is your character shaped through the actions and outlook required to maintain these relationships? If so, how?

6) God was clearly the ruler of Adam. How did God exercise His authority over Adam (vv. 2:16-17)? Did God yield authority to Adam (v. 2:19)? When a ruler yields authority, does that imply trust? Eph. 5:24 says that wives should submit to their husbands, which implies trust. Does God's example show that trust is intended to work both ways in a marriage?

7) Did Adam protect his wife from Satan's deceptive talk (v. 3:1-7)? Prior to eating from the tree of knowledge of good and evil, neither Adam nor Eve would have known about lying, deception, or the serpent's envious desires, and they would not have had a concept of loss, pain, and suffering. Other than the commandment from the Lord, would they have had any cause to perceive risk in listening to the serpent? Would they have been able to foresee the horrific personal consequences of their actions? When you follow the wisdom and commandments of God, do you do so only when you foresee potential negative consequences? At what point, will you be willing to simply trust in the Lord even when you, yourself, cannot conceive of any potentially negative consequences?

8) In v. 3:16, the word desire (*těshuwqah*, in Hebrew) is the same word used in v. 4:7, where it implies a longing to rule over an-

other. What are two possible interpretations of this desire in v. 3:16? In your experience, which seems right?

9) The second of the two grand analogies that God has repeatedly used to help describe our relationship with Him is that of God as our Father (Deut. 8:5, Deut. 32:6, Isa. 64:8, Hos. 11:1, Jer. 3:19, Mat. 3:17, Luke 12:29-32, Rom. 8:15). Some have argued that the God of the Old Testament is different from the God of the New Testament. Viewing our relationship with God using this parent analogy sheds new light on these differences. Read the short story, *A Parents Tale*, at the end of this section, and make a note of which aspects of the tale match the Biblical periods of God's redemptive story.

a) Adam the Garden before the fall:

b) Cain & Abel give offering to the Lord:

c) God gives Moses the Law:

d) The Israelites in the time of the Prophets:

e) Since Jesus fulfilled the Law through His death and resurrection:

10) In the opening of the short story, the children make a mess with ink. Why were they not in trouble for this? Romans 3:20 and 4:15 indicate that the Law brings knowledge of sin, and without this, there is no transgression. How is this concept similar to that of the tree of knowledge of good and evil (vv. 2:15-17, 3:22)? Once Adam and Eve ate of this fruit, did they become

aware of their transgressions (v. 3:7)? Does the Bible give any indication of whether or not Adam and Eve acted in maturity while in the Garden of Eden prior to their fall?

11) In vv. 2:16-17, was God threatening death as a punishment for eating the fruit, or was death a tragic consequence that God was warning Adam about? In this verse, was God warning about physical death, or spiritual death (e.g. a broken relationship with God)? How can our spiritual death be restored (John 3:16)?

12) The Hebrew word for skin, עוֹר (transliterated as ʿōr), is very similar to the Hebrew word for light, אוֹר (transliterated as ʾōr). Some Rabbinical scholars interpret meaning in this similarity as it relates to v. 3:21 *And the Lord God made for Adam and for his wife garments of skins and clothed them*, and they see it relating to the description of the skin on Moses' face shining (Ex. 34:29-35). Christians may also see a parallel to Matthew 5:16 *In the same way, let your light shine before others.* A few have speculated that this verse indicates that we were given earthly bodies, but most take this to mean that God literally created clothing made of animal skins. Some argue that this would necessitate God killing animals for their skin, and some have argued that God killed the serpent to obtain its skin. Does God have the power to create

animal skins without having to first create and then kill an animal? Some have argued that v. 3:21 shows that God performed the first sacrifice by killing an animal to obtain the skins, thus setting the standard for blood sacrifice. Does the actual story say one way or another how God came up with the skin or provide any more detailed description of the skin? If this incident was the cornerstone of the story of God's redemption of mankind, would you expect God to provide more detail?

13) In v. 2:17, God predicted an end to Adam's spiritual relationship with Him. After eating the apple, who was it that withdrew from the relationship (v. 3:8)? Many who come to know Christ late in life have difficulty accepting His forgiveness or entering in a relationship with Him because they are ashamed of past actions which, before knowing Christ, had never bothered their conscience. How does this compare with Adam and Eve's experience in v. 3:7? Adam and Eve attempted to hide their shame with fig leaves. What allegorical fig leaves have you used to hide your shame from God? Adam and Eve felt naked, and their feeling of nakedness caused them to draw away from God. What was God's response to this nakedness (v. 3:21)? What can we learn from this? What parallels exist between this action and the Gospel message of Christ?

14) In the short story, how tasty were the pancakes? Why were they appreciated? In vv 4:1-5, what distinguished Cain's offering (sacrifice) from Abel's? With possessions, we can satisfy our own desires and we can also bless others; what use we make of our possessions reveals our priorities in life (Luke 16:1-13). How do you think Cain and Abel prioritized their relationship with God?

15) Verses 4:1-5 are the first *explicit* mention of sacrifice in the Bible. Whose idea was it to make the sacrifice? For Abel, what do you think motivated this offering: was it that he thought that God would be hungry, or did he feel a need to give something up as a sign of contrition? Do you ever feel a need to give of yourself to make up for something you did wrong, even when what you give can't actually undo the wrong? Could God use this instinctual human trait to bring about good?

16) In corporate environments, managers often provide a documented set of job expectations, or performance goals, and then use these documented objectives as a basis for annual evaluations to appraise the value of the employee. Did God provide such a list of performance objectives for Cain and Abel? Does God follow the corporate model for evaluating us? If not, how

does he evaluate us?

17) In the first seven chapters of Leviticus as well as in Deuteronomy (Deut. 14:22-29), God gives specific commands on giving but in the story of Cain and Abel, God isn't valuing a sacrifice made out of obligation. What is the Spirit of giving that God values most (Ex. 35:29, 2 Cor. 9:7)? Why do you think God later felt the need to command giving?

18) In v. 4:5, Cain became angry with God. What made Cain so angry? When God asks us, or expects us, to do something, is it to satisfy and gratify His own needs, or ours? Have you ever been angry at God? Was your failure to live in the wisdom of God a root cause of whatever situation caused your anger?

19) What are the key points that God was trying to convey in vv. 2:4-4? What are your own key takeaways?

A Parents Tale

I remember when my boys were born. I don't think I had more than an hour's sleep a night for the first few weeks, but I loved them dearly. What rascals they were when they learned to move! The sound of my grandmother's crystal vase smashing was my first clue that they had learned to crawl, and it never occurred to me that that much ink could be in the fountain pen they discovered under the couch, but it was when they learned to walk, or run I should say, that our relationship began to change. You see, it was at this point, that I was no longer in complete control. We lived near a busy road and so they were given their first rule: *do not go near the street.* I impressed this rule upon then firmly, but it did not ease my fear. They were young and could not comprehend the horrible danger that lay a few feet beyond the yard. They loved me and they trusted me, but they yearned to explore the world on their own.

When they were about five, I was awoken on my birthday by a small, bright, flour-covered face bearing a plate of half-cooked pancakes—a present made especially for me. I had to forget a few of the rules that morning. As I sat enjoying the pancakes, his brother stopped in, saw the pancakes, took one last bite of a banana he was eating, and left me the rest. It's always so nice to feel appreciated.

As their sense of independence grew, it became apparent that it was time to lay down further ground rules for these young explorers. *Take off your muddy shoes when you come in the house, pick up your clothes,* and *do not talk back to your parents.* You'd think that we wouldn't have to spell them out. You'd think that they'd see muddy foot prints across the kitchen, but of course you wouldn't think this if you had kids of your own. We stenciled the rules on a little plaque that hung above the time-out corner.

The teen years were a struggle. There were times when I had to pull them back to save them from disaster, and other times, I reluctantly let them break free and do what they wished ... and wait for their pleaful cry when they came to realize that I was their only salvation.

It was hard when they finally left home. I raised them the best that I knew how, but they were now their own men and on their own. It was a few years later that I received my first call from either of them. One of my son's invited me to his place for Christmas. It seems that he met a girl that he wanted me to meet. What a day. And then, the following week, my other son shows up at my doorstep, wanting to visit for a couple of days. What a delightful surprise that was.

As it turns out, it wasn't so delightful. He stayed in his room most of the time, only coming down for meals. One morning, he didn't come down for breakfast, so I went to his room only to find his bed a mess and his bags gone, along with my TV. The second time it happened, I announced some conditions—he only stayed two nights, leaving with my heirloom silverware. The third time, I insisted that he get some help if he was going to stay—he just turned and left. The only news I heard of him after that was from the occasional police detective that dropped by to see if he was home.

The following Christmas, this sorrow was replaced with joy as I held my first granddaughter in my arms and the Christmas after that kept both arms full, with a grandson added to the mix. The laughter, chaos, and cheer in my home that morning warmed my soul. My heart was still singing when the doorbell rang. The smile on my face faded, as I opened the door. Pale, dirty, and with bloodshot eyes, stood my lost son. Just down the street idled a dented and rusting old car, out of which extended an arm that skillfully flicked a smoldering cigarette onto a neighbor's lawn. My son had brought friends. He said he'd come back later for supper, and could he borrow a few dollars—he'd pay me back soon. Behind me, I heard the pure laughter of children and the idle chit-chat of a son and new daughter who'd come home to be a part of my life. The threat of this lost son was no longer to me alone. It was no longer a choice and my heart was torn in two. I looked out at the shadow of the young man who I used to tickle in bed and carry on my shoulders. I looked out and said, I'm sorry, but I do not know you, and quietly closed the door.

29

GENESIS 5-23

The accounts of Noah and Abraham, in a sense, both represent new births. With Noah, all humanity was reborn through a baptismal flood and, with Abraham, a nation dedicated to God was born. These stories pass along to us both the theological underpinnings of our faith and the simple history, both good and bad, of Noah, Abraham, and their families. The nations that spring forth from the men of this generation will re-appear regularly in the story of the Semitic people as told in the remainder of the Old Testament. (The name *Semite* is derived from *Shem*, Noah's second born son.)

It is interesting to note that Noah and Abraham were the last men God selected exclusively because of their righteousness until the time of Joshua (Num. 27:18), and out of these men rose both the patriarchs of God's chosen people and the tribes that would grow to be both the snares and enemies of His chosen people for thousands of years to come.

Several years ago, a Chinese pastor asked Christians in America to stop praying for the persecution from his government to end, because his church was spiritually strengthened through its persecution. The early church was, likewise, strengthened under Roman persecution because such persecution forced believers to make a choice. Those with lukewarm faith (Rev. 3:16) left rather than stay where they would have served as a slow poison to those with true faith, and those with true faith learned to turn more fully to God, as Paul explains in Romans 5:3-5: *We rejoice in our sufferings, knowing that suffering produces endurance, and endurance produces character, and char-*

acter produces hope, and hope does not put us to shame, because God's love has been poured into our hearts through the Holy Spirit who has been given to us. In v. 16:12, God shares that Abraham's firstborn, Ishmael, *shall dwell over against all his kinsmen.* In v. 9:25, Noah curses Canaan to be servant of his brothers; likewise, in v. 25:23, God shares that Esau will serve Jacob. It is the descendents of these three men that embattle God's chosen people in the years to come, strengthening the Israelite's faith and unity as a people, and perhaps it is in this way that Canaan and Esau fulfilled their prophecy of service.

The level of detail in these histories is greater than that in the account of Adam, and these histories are related in a non-judgmental way, leaving it to the reader to discern whether or not the various anecdotes should serve as a model, or as a warning.

1) The genealogies in Genesis 5 reveal some astounding ages (see the section *Timeline of the Patriarchs*, at the front of this guide). A Bristlecone Pine tree was recently found to have lived over 5000 years. Certain clam species are known to live over 500 years, Bowhead whales have an average lifespan of about 200 years, and tortoises have been known to live over 200 years as well. Is it conceivable that a genetic variant would enable some humans to live hundreds of years?

2) Was Noah a perfect individual (vv. 9:20-27)? How did God view Noah (vv. 6:8-9, 2 Pet. 2:5, Heb. 11:7)? How did Noah's response to God's request compare with those of other prophets (Ex. 4:1,10, Jon. 1:1-3, Jer. 1:4-6)?

3) It must have taken a significant amount of time to build the ark. What do you think the neighbors thought about Noah and his project? Is it likely that he became the object or whispers, insults, and ridicules? Do those that follow the Lord have that same problem? How do you handle it? Do you ever hide your faith from others? What is it that you fear?

4) Why did God flood the earth (vv. 6:5-7)? How does our condition now compare with man's condition before the flood (Mat. 24:37-39, 2 Peter 2)?

5) What result of eating of the Tree of Knowledge of Good and Evil manifested itself in Noah's day (v. 6:5, Rom. 7:8)? When witnessing someone acting wickedly, say mugging an old woman or vandalizing property, many experience emotions of anger, disgust, and hatred. These are not the emotions God experienced (vv. 6:5-7), what were they and why did God feel the way He did? How can you shift your attitude and emotions to be more like God's when confronting others who are absorbed in sin? Was it man's *actions* alone that grieved God (v. 6:5, Mat. 5:22, 27-28)?

6) In vv. 3:17-19, we learn that God cursed the ground because Adam violated God's command and ate of the tree. Does vv. 8:20-21 imply that this curse has been eliminated? In vv. 5:28-29, we learn that Lamech named his son *Noah*, which means *rest* and which mirrors Lamech's explicit description of Noah's life purpose. Do you think Lamech's exclamation was a prayer, a prophecy, a child dedication, or an exercise of a God given authority (See also Matt. 13:31)?

7) What two rules did God give Noah (9:4-7)? Jackals, wild dogs, and snapping turtles will take bites out of animals while they are still alive (and fighting). Why do you think God prohibited man from doing the same (Deut. 12:13, Lev. 17:11)?

8) *Covenant*, simply means *contract*. In vv. 9:8-17, God makes his first covenant with man. What were terms of this contract?

9) In vv. 9:24-27, Noah cursed Ham's son Canaan. Was Noah's response justifiable? In later passages of the Bible, we learn more of the practices of the Canaanite tribes (Deut. 18:9-14, Gen. 15:16), and archeological evidence indicates that these tribes worshipped multiple gods and incorporated both sexuality (v. 38:21) and child sacrifice in their religious practices. What might have turned Canaan away from the God who had just spared his own father from the flood? How powerful is the impact of a father's, and grandfather's words on a young man? How did your own father's words influence you? If you are a father, how much care do you put into the words you speak to your children?

10) While God did rescue Noah because he found him righteous, God's call to Abram (vv. 12:1-4) is the first time that God calls out an individual for a special purpose. Was Abram perfect (12:13)?

The ancient Near East civilization, at the time of Abraham, was polytheistic, with people worshipping many gods. There were personal clan gods, who were associated with the household; regional gods associated with a particular city or area; and major gods, who controlled the Earth and sky. These gods needed to be constantly appeased to avoid their wrath or curry their favors, and idols and temples were created to provide places for the gods to inhabit. When God revealed Himself to Abram, Abram's first instinct, undoubtedly, would have been to attempt to fit God into one of his understood categories of godly beings. As you work through the remaining chapters, it is worth exploring the ways in which God revealed His unique qualities to Abram, Isaac, and Jacob, as well as the ways in which He refrained from exposing His full nature.

11) In v. 12:1, God asks Abram to leave his family. Why do you think God wanted to separate Abram from his people, and do you think it was emotionally difficult for Abram to do? Did he do it anyway? What were Abram's priorities? Is it possible that we too, should separate from old friends and family in order to grow in our relationship with God?

12) What three promises does God make to Abraham (vv. 12:2-3, 12:7)?

13) In vv. 12:10-13:7, we learn that, due to famine, Abram went to Egypt, but God used plagues to rescue him and his wife, and he came out with riches given by Pharaoh. Abram then moved from place to place, eventually settling in the land of Canaan that God promised him (vv. 13:12, 23:19-20). What future event does this foreshadow (Exodus)? Did Abram learn his lesson in regard to how he treats his wife (Gen. 20)?

14) Verses 14:17-20 introduce us to Melchizedek of Salem (Salem later came to be called Jerusalem), who blesses Abram and offers bread and wine to sustain him. What does this foreshadow (Heb. 5:5-6, 7:1-3, Mark 14:22-25)? Why did Abram give Melchizedek a tenth of everything?

15) What did Abram have to do to be declared righteous (v. 15:6, Rom. 4)? Was God's prophecy (vv. 15:12-16) a response to Abram's questioning of God (v. 15:8)?

16) Does God always punish sin right away (v. 15:16, 18:32, Rom. 1:25-32, 2:5-10)? Why? Does He ever choose to simply overlook sin?

17) In our individualistic culture, we view sin as personal and see it as righteous when rewards or consequences are assigned to each individual in accordance with their attitudes and behavior. The Mesopotamian culture was a communal one, where families and cities felt a collective responsibility for each other's attitudes and behavior. Which of these philosophies does God appear to be reflecting in Gen. 15:14-16 and 18:20-21? How do you think God will judge your current family and society? Do you feel any responsibility towards influencing your family's or your society's moral standing? Which of the two philosophies toward sin (personal or communal), seems most justified to you, and why?

18) What are the terms of God's covenant with Abram (v. 15:17-21, 17:4-14)? What makes someone an offspring of Abraham and an inheritor of this covenant (Mat. 3:9, Rom. 4:13-25)?

19) Why was it significant, to the people in Moses' day, that God changed Abram's and Sarai's names (vv. 17:5,15)?

20) Does *The Angel of the Lord* (vv. 16:7-13) assert the prerogatives of the Lord? Does He accept being identified as God? How does this compare with Paul's and Barnabas' reaction to being called a god (Acts 14:11-14), or Herod's (Acts 12:21-23)? Christians often describe the various manifestations of God as a trinity (Yahweh the Father, Jesus the son, and the Holy Spirit). Is *The Angel of the Lord* a fourth? What was the purpose of this first recorded visit of The Angel of the Lord? What was the station, or class, of the person whom the Angel first visited? Who did Jesus come to visit (Mat. 9:10)? Some scholars suggest that The Angel of the Lord is the pre-incarnate Jesus noting that The Angel of the Lord has not appeared since Jesus' coming and also noting similarities in the ministries of The Angel and Christ. Do you think this view is justifiable?

21) In vv. 18:9-15, Sarai laughs at the notion that she would be blessed with a child. In what ways have you lived with discouragement for so long that it has become part of your sense of self? Does it have to be?

22) Most would agree that God can do anything on His own, and we often expect God to work this way; however, the Bible indicates that God frequently seeks to work in partnership with man (Josh. 6:1-5, Jud. 6:11-16, Mat. 9:37, 28:16-20). The NIV translates Gen. 18:19 using the word *will*, which implies a contractual type of arrangement, but most translations use the word *may*, which suggests that living a life of righteousness and justice *enables* God to bless us. Who would you think would feel more blessed by God, members of a community in which everyone acts to fulfill their own selfish lusts and desires, or one in which members act in the spirit of the Ten Commandments? Partnerships work when both parties work in unity. What wisdom does God provide for bring about unity (Job 22:21, Prov. 3:5-6, Eph. 5:21-23, 1 Pet. 5:5, Mat. 6:10, Luke 22:42)? In your own life, have you ever experience blessings that were a direct result of your walk in faith? Could the converse be true, are you losing out on blessings because your lack of faith has not properly prepared you to receive them?

23) In v. 18:17, it sounds as if the Lord wanted to provide a management training lesson for the man He had just chosen to launch His nation. What lesson(s) do you believe the Lord wanted to teach Abraham and, how would you rate Abraham's response?

24) Frequently in the Bible, we find the Lord chastising men who question Him (Job 38, Luke 1:18-20). In vv. 18:22-33, Abraham repeatedly questions God without experiencing any correction or retribution. What was Abraham's attitude toward God in this questioning? What was Abraham's motivation for risking this confrontation? What can we learn from this in regard to our own interactions with God?

25) Within the Canaanite culture, sacrificing children to appease the gods was an established practice. Is it possible that the Lord wanted to know if Abraham was willing to make the same level of sacrifice for Him (vv. 22:1-19)?

26) Abraham was 100 years old when Isaac was born (v. 21:5), and Isaac was old enough to carry enough wood up a mountain to consume a sacrifice (vv. 22:1-13). Do you think Isaac could have escaped Abraham's grasp, as Abraham bound him? Do you think that both Abraham and Isaac showed great faith that day? How would you describe Abraham's priorities? What other Biblical character carried wood for their own sacrifice (John 19:16-17)? Did God provide the sacrificial lamb, as Abraham predicted (vv. 22:8, 13, John 1:29)?

Note: Some Archeological evidence suggests that Jesus was crucified on Mt. Moriah: this very same mountain.

27) Who will be blessed because of Abraham's faith (Gen. 22:18)?

28) What are the key lessons of the story of Abraham?

GENESIS 24-36

Genesis 24 through 36 provide us with a story of three shepherds: Isaac and Jacob, as they guided their flocks through the land, and the Lord, as He guided Isaac and Jacob through their lives. More can be gained from these stories, however, if we see in them an account of the rocky start of a marriage between God and His chosen people. A marriage that would end in divorce (Jer. 3:8) many years later.

Love, within the marriage context, goes through phases. In the first, couples are enamored with each other and see no faults. In the final phase, reached only by couples who develop intimacy, partners agree to stick with each other and love each other in spite of their faults. God's marriage with His people was initiated with the Lord's covenant with Abraham in Gen. 17, whom He found righteous (v.15:6). As you read the accounts of Isaac and Jacob, make note of how God touched their lives even though their faults were evident. Does God seek intimacy? Does God offer guidance and protection? Is God steadfast in His love for His new bride in spite of their failures? How do Isaac and Jacob respond to this? Are they always trusting in the Lord? Are they faithful to God alone? Do they grow to be more like Him?

1) Why did Abraham not want his son to marry a local girl (vv. 24:1-6, 1 Kings 11:4 , 2 Cor. 6:14)? Did Abraham's family know the Lord (vv. 24:50-51)? Why did Abraham feel that Isaac must not go back to his family? How would you describe the qualities

of a girl who might fulfill the servant's prayer (vv. 24:12-14)?

2) In Gen. 24, the events surrounding Rebekah at the well are detailed out four times (vv. 24:12-14, 15-20, 42-44, 45-46). Why did the author espouse this event so much?

3) Many people within the encampment of Abraham could have kept Isaac company. What does the tail end of verse 24:67 tell us about human relationships? What needs of a man does both a wife and mother meet? How should a man's relationship with, and expectations of, his wife and mother differ?

4) In v. 26:3, God directs a patriarch to sojourn in a land of foreign gods and evil ways. What does it mean to sojourn? Did God hope that their experience as a sojourner would develop a

sense of compassion for others (Lev. 19:34, Zech. 7:10)? Are we, as the body of Christ, also sojourners in a land of foreign gods and evil ways (John 17:14-19)? If so, what do you believe God wants us to learn?

5) In Matthew 25:35-40, Jesus taught that the righteous will feed a hungry stranger. How would you describe the character of Jacob (vv. 25:29-34, 27:11-12, 27:35, 29:31-32, 30:28-43, 33:2)? In Gen. 26, we learn that Isaac had gained great might to the point where other nations felt threatened by his power (v. 26:16). How did Isaac handle this power (vv. 26:17-31)?

6) What can we discern from vv. 27:5-14 and 27:42-46 about Rebekah's character? What might have caused Rebekah to lose respect for Isaac (vv. 26:6-7)?

7) In vv. 25:29-34, we learn that Esau didn't make great decisions, but what can we discern of Esau's character from vv. 28:6-9, 33:4?

8) In ancient Mesopotamia, many cities had Ziggurats, or tall temples with stairways leading up to the top. Jacob's vision, in vv. 28:10-22, describes angels ascending and descending on a ladder (or stairway), which is reflective of these Ziggurats. Jewish scholars have noted an interesting contrast between this vision and the account of the Tower of Babel as described in vv. 11:1-9. In each story, who initiated this bridge between heaven and earth? What was the attitude, or motivation, of the people of Babel? What was the motivation for God? Prior to building the Tower of Babel, were the people united? Prior to Jacob's vision, was he in union with his family? In regard to unity, how do the stories end (vv. 11:8, 28:14)? All of us are in need of a restored connection with God. How do these two stories help us understand the source of lasting restoration? (See also Rom. 10:6.)

9) In v. 28:18, Jacob setup a stone pillar and anointed it. He did the same thing again, in v. 35:14, at the command of God. Why then does God forbid the setting up of pillars in Lev. 26:1 and Deut. 16:22 (Rom. 14:2-6)? Is it specific *actions*, such as setting

up a pillar, that God finds hurtful or something deeper?

10) When confronted with a new concept, most of us attempt to force the new idea into the framework of our previously existing knowledge. In Jacob's pantheistic society, most gods were local or family gods that demanded to be served, rather than to serve. Do you think God, as he revealed himself to Jacob in vv. 28:10-15, fit well in this pantheistic framework? In v. 28:20, Jacob appears to be negotiating a deal with God, as if he simply cannot believe that a *god,* or any of the gods, would really do this for him. Why did God not act in anger towards Jacob in his disbelief as he did when Zechariah questioned the angel (in Luke 1:18-20)? Does God have patience with you, when you don't fully understand how He is trying to work in your life?

11) How is Leah compared with her sister Rachel (v. 29:16)? Rachel, the younger daughter, was obviously of marrying age when Jacob met her seven years prior to his marriage to Leah. What level of confidence did Laban have that another man would come along and desire Leah? How do you think Leah felt, always being compared to her younger and more beautiful sister? When, in your own life, have you felt lacking or substandard as compared to someone else? Who may feel substandard

as they compare themselves to you? (If so, how actively do you seek to encourage them?)

Marriage, in ancient Mesopotamia, was a business arrangement, initiated with a contract between a man and the bride's father, and it was not uncommon for the bride and groom to have never met. The Mesopotamians considered marriage a key component of an orderly society, with a marriage's primary purpose being that of extending the family line. A marriage became official upon consummation, and failure of a girl to get pregnant was grounds for divorce. Thus, within the marriage context, rights and honor due to a women were based on her *position* as the wife, rather than on any *affection* a man may have had for her. (Although historical evidence shows that love and affection were often an outgrowth of marriage.) It was common, in that time, for the first wife to participate in the selection of subsequent wives, and it was the first wife's duty to insure that subsequent wives met their responsibilities, within the household.

12) What do you think Leah's emotional state was, when she agreed to go along with her father's deception (vv. 29:21-26)? How do you think she felt over the next two weeks (vv. 29:27-30)? What was it that Leah most desired (vv. 29:32, 29:30) that she received neither from her father nor from her husband? Compare the names of Leah's first three children with the name of her fourth. What inward change do think caused this shift in her heart? What do you derive your sense of worth from?

13) What does v. 31:19 tell us of Rachel's character? Had Jacob establish a tone of integrity within his family (v. 31:20)?

14) In Gen. chapters 31 and 32, we find that Jacob has left Laban after hearing that Laban felt cheated by Jacob (vv. 31:1-2), just as Jacob felt cheated by Laban (v. 31:7) and finds himself on a collision course with his brother Esau, who felt twice cheated by Jacob (v. 27:36). What emotions does Jacob experience at this situation (vv. 32:7-8)? Did the Lord anticipate Jacob's anxiety and provide for him any sign of encouragement (v. 32:1)?

15) Jacob implements a two phase plan for dealing with the situation: prayer (vv. 32:9-11) and bribery (vv. 32:13-21). How does Jacob's understanding of righteousness, as revealed in this prayer, compare with his approach to living? Did Jacob's attempt at bribery reveal a lack in faith in God, or does God expect us to engage our full mind, soul, heart, and strength to life's challenging situations in conjunction with our prayer?

16) In the story of Jacob's life, from birth through his breaking away from Laban, it is clear that God reached out to Jacob (vv. 28:10-22), but did Jacob ever reach out to, and put his trust in, God? Up until this point in Jacob's life, he appears to have navigated life reasonably successfully through his lies and deception, but as he leaves Laban's, this is no longer the case. God attempted to get Jacob's attention through the visitation of an angel (v. 32:1), but Jacob continued to rely on his own devices. In v. 32:24, we find that Jacob is in fear of his life from his brother Esau and is now alone–separated from his wives, children, servants, and all his possessions. In this, Jacob's darkest moment, what did God do, to finally get Jacob's attention vv. 32-24-25?

17) Within this chapter, the author of Genesis does not specifically declare the *man* to be God, but it is clear from vv. 32:28 that Jacob believed him to be so. Hos. 12:4 indicates that the *man* was an angel. If so, it is clear that he spoke with the authority of God, as did the angel of God that appeared in vv. 31:11-12. How is it that the *man* could not prevail against Jacob all night but, with a simple touch, could put out Jacob's hip socket? Many verses indicate God's power (psalm 62:11, Job 26:1-14), how is it conceivable that a mere human could prevail against Him (John 19)? How would you relate this physical struggle with God, with Jacob's Spiritual struggle with God?

18) When a young man asks the father of a girl he wishes to marry for his blessing, he is both asking for something that he wants and, at the same time, placing himself in humble subjugation to the father. By asking for this blessing, he is seeking to establish a relationship with the father, founded upon a sense of conveyed honor. Is the question Jacob asks, in v. 32:26, a question that God has been waiting for Jacob to ask? Recall that within this ancient culture, there was a notion that a person's name defined their nature, and if someone knew your real name, they might have control over you. With this in mind, what is the *man* really asking Jacob (v. 32:27) when he asks *What is your name?* When Jacob, in turn, asks for the *man's* name (v. 32:29), do you think he is seeking control over the man, or seeking to understand, better, who he is?

19) After this exchange, did Jacob finally submit his full heart to the Lord, or did he continue to wrestle? Have you ever wrestled with God, knowing He's there, but wanting to do things your own way? How long does God allow you to wrestle with Him, even when you think you are winning?

Bible translators and commentators have viewed Gen. 34 in different ways. The original Hebrew word, *anah* (meaning *to humble a woman by cohabitation*) (v. 34:2), has been translated with varying (and possibly incorrect) connotations as *humiliated, defiled, layed with by force,* and *raped.* The original Hebrew word, *tame* (meaning *to be or become unclean*) (v. 34:27), is translated consistently as *defiled.* At the time, women were considered to be of marrying age at puberty, and historians believe that Dinah was likely thirteen to fifteen years old but may have been older. In the culture, marriages traditionally were arranged business deals between parents, and the love or desires of the bride and groom were not necessarily considered. One method of subverting such arrangements, was for a young couple to covertly engage in sex. While the act would be considered a defilement, the parents often felt compelled to allow the marriage. Following the Israelites exodus from Egypt, the Lord provided Moses with commandments for these situations (Ex. 22:16-17, Dt: 22:28-29).

20) Did Dinah's mother use deceptive sex to secure her own marriage? Is it conceivable that Dinah, daughter of the wife that Jacob didn't love and the only daughter among twelve brothers, would have a longing for attention and affection? Could such a girl succumb to sweet-talk and manipulation by a prince (v. 34:3)? If you have daughters, are you sure that they are secure in your love and affection for them? From the time that Jacob first heard of Dinah's humiliation, how long was it that she stayed in Shechem's home (vv. 34:25-26)? Did the prince seem like the kind of boy who is used to getting what he wants (v. 34:4)?

21) Whether the humiliation was perpetrated through physical force or through sweet-talking, it violated the customs of the day, and it is clear that all parties understood that it was wrong. Did Hamor and Shechem attempt to make things right (v. 34:6-12)? What did Hamor offer? What did he expect to get (v. 34:23)?

22) Who plotted the deception against Hamor's people (v. 34:13)? Who carried it out (v. 34:25)? Who benefited from the murders (v. 34:27)? Was Jacob most concerned about the safety and honor of his daughter or something else (v. 34:30)? Do you think Simeon and Levi (also children of Leah) had respect for their father in regard to his care of their sister (v. 34:31)? What did Jacob think of them (vv. 34:5-7)? How do you view the actions of the characters in this story, did any act in righteousness? Who was responsible for their behaviors? Was Dinah the only child of Jacob guilty of sexual sin (v. 35:22, vv. 38:15-19)?

23) When God told Jacob to leave Laban, where did he tell Jacob to go (v. 31:13)? Where did Jacob tell Esau he would go after they met on his journey (v. 33:14)? Where did Jacob actually go (vv. 33:17-18)? How did his failure to listen to the Lord's direction work out for his family?

24) What was God's response to Jacob's situation (v. 35:1)? Was Jacob aware that his wives and members of his households worshipped other gods (vv. 35:2-4)? Why do you think he decided, at this time, to purge them? Did God remain committed to His promises to Jacob (vv. 35:5-13)? Would it be fair for Jacob to ask how God could allow such evil in the world? In v. 18:19,

God said: *For I have chosen him, that he may command his children and his household after him to keep the way of the LORD by doing righteousness and justice, so that the LORD may bring to Abraham what he has promised him* (ESV). By failing to trust in the Lord, and failing to live in righteousness, was God hindered in his ability to protect Jacob and bless him?

25) Was God's plan for Isaac's and Jacob's lives intended to bless Isaac and Jacob alone (v. 26:4, 28:14)? Were Isaac and Jacob perfect, saint-like men? Do you think that it is possible that God has a plan for your life too? Would you be excited, or disappointed, to learn that His plan for your life might be intended to bless others and not just you, yourself? Have you ever been reluctant to put yourself in service for God because you felt that you are *not good* enough to be used effectively by Him?

26) What are the key lessons of the story of Isaac and Jacob?

GENESIS 37-50

The story of Joseph represents another grand turning point in God's redemptive plan for His people. For the first time in history, we encounter a man who goes out of his way to extend unearned mercy and abounding kindness to those who persecuted him unjustly. And not only does Joseph extend such mercy to his brothers, he does it in a deeply thoughtful and methodical way that, while it caused him additional suffering, was intended to enable his brothers to fully accept the forgiveness granted to them, a pattern reflective of God's plan of reconciliation that culminated with Jesus' death on the cross.

Joseph's story, at the same time, reveals God's hand in history, marshaling people and events as a master chess player marshals knights and rooks. In one fluid sequence, God introduces forgiveness and mercy, saves His people from starvation, draws the brothers into tighter unity, and brings them to Egypt where enslavement would keep them isolated and unified for 400 years so that they could grow into a nation ready to hear His law: the law that would serve as their guardian and tutor (Gal. 3:24) until the time of Christ.

1) Did Joseph endear himself to his brothers (vv. 37:1-2)? Did Jacob do anything to help bring a spirit of love and unity amongst his sons (v. 37:3:4)? Did God (vv. 37:5-11)?

2) When stories are told, irrelevant details are usually left out, and stories passed down through generations are particularly susceptible to the pruning of irrelevant detail. Verses 37:15-17, therefore, are particularly intriguing. Were they included because they represent the first (and perhaps only) time the Bible records a man asking for directions? (Was this an indication of humility in Joseph?) How would the course of human history be different if this man had not been in the field at this particular time? Who might the man have been (vv. 32:24)? How much pain and torment would Joseph have avoided if the man had not been there? (A timeline can be gauged with v. 37:2 and v. 41:46.)

3) Joseph's murder would be wrong and his death would certainly cause great sorrow and heartache for their father. Why might Reuben have had more sensitivity and compassion than his brothers (vv. 37:21-22, v. 35:22)?

4) Chapter 38 opens with *It happened at that time*. What might have motivated Judah to leave home shortly after witnessing his father's grief over the loss of Joseph (Adullam is south of Dothan, where the brothers had been pasturing their flocks)? In v. 37:24-25, the brothers were comfortable enough with their

treachery to enjoy lunch. Have you ever noticed a difference in how you feel about your own selfishness when you are forced to witness the suffering of those you have sinned against? Have you ever gone out of your way to avoid being around those you've sinned against just so that you don't have to see the pain? Do you go out of your way to visualize the likely pain of others prior to doing something selfish?

5) Why did Joseph refuse to sleep with Potiphar's wife (vv. 39:6-18,1 Cor. 6:18)? Who did he not want to hurt? Who did he see as his judge? Did Joseph's brothers consider the fact that they would be judged for their sinful actions?

6) A primary reason for world hunger today is not lack of grain but the fact that competing tribes want their neighbors to starve and die. (The idea that Egypt's neighboring nations were considered potential threats is clear from v. 42:9.) Why, then, did Joseph allow his fixed supply of grain to be sold to people from other nations (vv. 47:13-26)?

7) Joseph was a highly gifted individual. Did he see his success as being a result of his own hard work and tough experiences (v. 41:16)? What do you credit your own successes to? Joseph was handsome (v. 39:6), shrewd (vv. 41:33, 47:20-21), and trusted (v. 39:4, 39:22, 41:39-41). Who benefited from Joseph's gifts, skills, and hard work? For whose benefit do you apply your skills, talents, and energy? What attitude do you think Joseph embodied (Col. 3:23, Eph. 6:5-9)?

8) Joseph was unquestionably an all-powerful ruler in the land of Egypt where Reuben, Judah, and his brothers found themselves as they went in search for food, and he made it clear that atonement would be demanded for any transgressions against Pharaohs house (v. 42:18, 28, 44:10). Unbeknownst to his brothers, Joseph actually had tremendous compassion for them and a great longing to have a restored relationship with them. Prior to offering any forgiveness, though, Joseph gave them time to reflect and be repentant for that they'd done. Where else in the Bible does a similar scenario show itself (Luke 24:45-47?

9) Reuben had evidently left the company of his brothers when Joseph was sold into slavery. Who was the next oldest brother

(vv. 29:31-33)? In v. 42:22, the brother's realized that a reckoning was due for their sin against Joseph. Who did Joseph hold as ransom (v. 42:24)? Who offered the lives of his own sons as security for the return of Benjamin (v. 42:37)? Who actually sold Joseph into slavery (v. 37:26-27)? Who offered his own life in place of Benjamin's (vv. 44:18-33)? Which of the brothers had carried the largest burdens of guilt for their sin against Joseph and their father? Who received emotional healing when Simeon, Reuben, and Judah took responsibility for their past sins and accepted the consequences of their sins? If Joseph had revealed himself the first day the brothers showed up in Egypt and immediately offered his forgiveness, would the brothers ever truly felt restored? Why does God demand atonement for our sins (Ex. 16, Rom. 3:25,6:23), is it because He is vindictive, or something else?

10) In v. 44:12, Benjamin was caught with a stolen cup, a crime punishable by slavery or death. Why would Judah, who was innocent of this crime, offer to substitute himself for Benjamin (v. 44:33), accepting slavery as atonement for Benjamin's crime? Was Judah's self-sacrifice a foreshadowing of other events in God's plan of redemption (1 Pet. 3:18)? From which of Jacob's sons did Jesus descend (Mat. 1:1-17)?

11) Joseph's strategy for reuniting with his brothers was complex and played out over an extended period of time. Could the depth of healing between himself and his brothers been accomplished any other way? Could the brothers have come to accept themselves again in any other way? The sins of the world are many, and our own sins are many. In what ways does the story of Joseph help you to have a greater appreciation for those works of God that enable our internal and relational healing? In what areas could you put a greater depth of thought into how you bring healing to others? When you forgive, do you take steps to insure that the other person feels forgiven? When forgiveness is offered to you, do you accept it and insure that your acceptance is known? To what extent have you been willing to give your life up (Mark 8:35, 1 John 3:16)?

12) The brothers had taken various roles in the enslavement of Joseph and now, for the first time, they are going to have to tell their father what they did. What did Joseph say to minimize the consequences of this (v. 45:24)? When you are caught in wrongdoing or failure with others, is your first inclination to accept personal responsibility or is it to think about all the ways that other's coerced you to participate, focusing on their role in the event?

13) Jacob, his sons, and large extended family could have been perceived as either a burden or a threat to the Egyptians, and immigrating into a powerful, paganist society put the Israelites at risk, spiritually. Did Joseph anticipate these risks? What did Joseph say to minimize the risk of his family being perceived as a burden (v. 47:1)? What did Joseph do to minimize any perceived threat his family may have faced and, at the same time, maintain maximum isolation for his people (vv. 46:31-34)? Where the Israelites, in fact, ever perceived as a threat (Ex. 1:8-14)?

14) Jacob deceived his father, cheated his brother, failed to love his first wife and his children as a man should, cheated his father-in-law, and lied to his brother after they were re-united. In v. 47:9, Jacob used the Hebrew word *Ra`*, to describe his life. *Ra`* has been translated as *difficult, unpleasant,* or *painful,* but in v. 47:9, it is most often translated as *evil.* Psychologists have noted that most of us have a natural tendency to project our goals, values, feelings, and behaviors on others. How might this tendency explain Jacob's assessment of his life? How many men, in recorded history, have had as many face-to-face encounters with the Lord as Jacob did? How many have received such blessing from the Lord? How do you view your life? How have the choices you've made in life, colored your impression of it? Which do you notice more, the evil or the blessings?

15) As Jacob neared the end of his days, it seems hard to image that he was not thinking back on his own father's blessing as he reached out to bless the two children of Joseph (Gen. 48). Genesis is unclear as to why Jacob chose to put his primary blessing on Joseph's second born, rather than the more traditional first-born son. What possible reasons might there have been for this (v. 41:51)? What other first-borns, in Genesis, failed to be honored (vv. 3:17, 4:3-12, 17:20-21, 38:27-30, 1 Cor. 15:45-47)? In the ancient culture, first-borns were most honored (v. 49:3) and normally received a double portion of inheritance. Why does God seem to make a point of denying the privilege due to these first-borns?

16) Did Jacob's blessing to his sons (v. 49:2-27) reveal a spirit of love and forgiveness? How accurate where his prophetic words about Judah? To what do each of the lines of this prophecy refer (vv. 49:10-12)?

17) When Joseph first revealed himself to his brothers, he quite obviously forgave them and, in fact, fed them, stuffed their bags with valuables, saved their entire families from starvation, and gave them a safe new homeland. Are people who do evil, more likely to expect others to do evil to them? After Jacob's death,

what did the brothers expect from Joseph (v. 50:15)? Was Joseph hurt by the fact that they had not yet accepted his forgiveness (v. 50:17)? What did he do to help them accept his forgiveness (v. 50:19-21)? What does your expectation from others tell you about yourself? Has it ever occurred to you that failure to fully accept the grace and forgiveness from others, and from God may cause them pain? Is it selfish to continue to think of yourself as unworthy, or refuse to accept this kind of love from others? Is it selfish to think that you have no need for anyone's forgiveness?

18) What do you see as the major themes and lessons of the story of Jacob? How can you apply these in your own life?

19) What do you see as the major themes and lessons of Genesis, as a whole?

DEDICATION

This book is dedicated to the incarcerated men, women, and children of our society who wonder, because of the past choices they've made or the place where they now live, if God can still have a purpose and plan for their lives. Who wonder if God still cares about them, and who may even wonder if anyone outside their walls cares about them. My fervent hope and prayer is that through a study of Genesis, the Spirit will reveal to you the truthful answers of yes, yes, and yes.